indivisible

Poems for Social Justice

Foreword by
COMMON

Edited by
Gail Bush & Randy Meyer

*To Face-lt,
with a patient
confidence,*

*Gail Bush.
2013.*

NORWOOD HOUSE PRESS
CHICAGO, ILLINOIS

Acknowledgments & Dedication

We are grateful to many who have joined us along the way to help bring this anthology to you. We have worked on *Indivisible* for the lifetime of an adolescent now and it would still be a project searching for a home if it were not for the generous support and encouragement of Patti Hall, founder and president of Norwood House Press. Thanks to National Louis University graduate assistant Katie Wooten who spent hours learning about the childhoods of our poets.

We thank COMMON and the Common Ground Foundation, who contributed the heartfelt foreword and a wellspring of support. Our deep appreciation to Matthew Thomas Bush for his continuous lines of illustration that grace this book and so elegantly represent our vision, and to Claire Steinglass for setting her renowned networking skills into motion on behalf of this project.

Together we dedicate this labor of love to America's youth, wherever they may roam, and especially to Phoebe.

—G.B. & R.M.

Norwood House Press
PO Box 316598
Chicago, IL 60631
www.norwoodhousepress.com

Illustrator: Matthew Thomas Bush
Designer: Kathy Petelinsek

Library of Congress Cataloging-in-Publication Data

Indivisible : poems for social justice / edited by Gail Bush and Randy Meyer [editors].
     p. cm.
  Summary: "Anthology including over 50 works of poetry by 20th century writers on issues related
to social justice in American society. Foreword by COMMON"— Provided by publisher.
  Includes bibliographical references and index.
  ISBN 978-1-60357-417-4 (pbk. : alk. paper) 1. Social problems—Poetry.
2. Social justice—Poetry. I. Bush, Gail. II. Meyer, Randy.
  PS595.S75I53 2012
  811.008'03556—dc23
                        2012021600

For information on educational sales, please call our customer service department at 866-565-2900.
©2013 by Gail Bush
Manufactured in The United States of America in Peoria, Illinois. 232R—042013.

Table of Contents

liberty was misquoted

we are all getting burned

giving secrets away

the signals we give

the next thing to happen

Foreword

As we read in the Introduction, the editors tell us that the idea of America takes work, that we have a difficult time matching our words with our deeds. As an instrument of my deeds, I started the Common Ground Foundation because I wanted to help. *Indivisible: Poems for Social Justice* fits my mission perfectly. My driving passion is to help people to help themselves. There are poems included in this anthology for people in every margin of our society. By seeing themselves in these poems, they can first reflect back and then look ahead to where they want to see themselves in the future. And, by engaging with the poems about others, they can relate to experiences foreign to their own. They will have a more understanding appreciation of the parallel journey taken as we fight the good fight, with liberty and justice for all.

I always believed that if we started with the youth then we would be planting the seeds for our future to blossom. That philosophy is in action in our Lighthouse Youth Center and our Summer Youth Camp programs in Chicago, which are realizations that at the Common Ground Foundation we do believe strongly in the power of the message to youth, especially to our urban youth. These poems will teach also those who work with our youth to help understand them better. In fact, they have something to teach us all regardless of our stage of life, where we might reside now or where we are headed. So while I do believe in giving the children a sense of hope, self-esteem, and love that will better the world, I think that we all need that embrace to feel safe to live our lives and to follow the golden rule with each other.

I think making a difference in the lives of others is life's greatest purpose. I walk this path with faith knowing that the Common Ground Foundation will change the world. With *Indivisible: Poems for Social Justice*, the editors have created a vehicle for the words of our most cherished and some lesser known American poets to send a message that we might translate into hope and love. We believe you will appreciate that *Indivisible: Poems for Social Justice* is a shared message that is fitting our one nation as we continue to do the hard work, together.

COMMON
Chicago, Illinois

Introduction

America is not easy. It's a land of high ideals and stirring icons, but it is also a land of harsh realities. We celebrate the incredible achievements of individuals as we turn our gaze from hunger and homelessness in the streets. We have a difficult time matching our words with our deeds.

This is where poetry comes in. A poem has the ability to personalize the ideal, to make it tangible in a way that a speech or news report cannot. It can widen the angle through which we view society. It can move us to action.

We selected the poems in this anthology because they do just that: confront, challenge, and inspire. They take us on a journey toward social justice, starting in the shadows and slowly working our way home. Beginning with "liberty was misquoted" we see from the outside the challenges America presents. "We are all getting burned" takes us a step closer, introducing us to communities outside our own. And in "giving secrets away" we look inside those communities to understand people's lives through their own eyes, to walk in their shoes.

After traveling down a road riddled with conflict, the journey takes us inside our own thoughts as we begin to link our dream with the dreams of others. In "the signals we give" we share experiences, we acknowledge our strengths and weaknesses. "The next thing to happen" connects us under a shared sky to the mutual triumphs and failures as equal members of the human race. Our dream expressed with different voices singing the same song, traveling down the same road home.

These poems have been selected and arranged and offered to the reader as our contributions to living in a more socially just America. We have done our part with the blessings of these fine poets. Now it's your turn. Read, re-read aloud, think, feel, discuss, reject, reflect, reconsider. Repeat with those poems that speak directly to you. And for those poems that make you think about how you breathe, keep those especially close to your heart.

Gail Bush   *Randy Meyer*
Evanston, Illinois   *Somerville, Massachusetts*

Why should there not be a patient confidence
in the ultimate justice of the people?
Is there any better or equal hope in the world?

Abraham Lincoln, First Inaugural Address

liberty was misquoted

Immigrants
Nancy Byrd Turner

"These foreigners with strange and avid faces
Crowding our shores, marring our pleasant places,
They must be curbed...." So mused King Powhatan,
Hundred per cent, red-blood American.

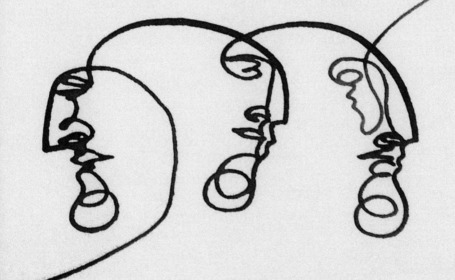

Enemies

Wendell Berry

If you are not to become a monster,
you must care what they think.
If you care what they think,

how will you not hate them,
and so become a monster
of the opposite kind? From where then

is love to come – love for your enemy
that is the way of liberty?
From forgiveness. Forgiven, they go

free of you, and you of them;
they are to you as sunlight
on a green branch. You must not

think of them again, except
as monsters like yourself,
pitiable because unforgiving.

the ISM

Wanda Coleman

tired i count the ways in which it determines my life
permeates everything. it's in the air
lives next door to me in stares of neighbors
meets me each day in the office. its music comes out the radio
drives beside me in my car. strolls along with me
down supermarket aisles
it's on television
and in the streets even when my walk is casual/undefined
it's overhead flashing lights
i find it in my mouth
when i would speak of other things

Discrimination

Kenneth Rexroth

I don't mind the human race.
I've got pretty used to them
In these past twenty-five years.
I don't mind if they sit next
To me on streetcars, or eat
In the same restaurants, if
It's not at the same table.
However, I don't approve
Of a woman I respect
Dancing with one of them. I've
Tried asking them to my home
Without success. I shouldn't
Care to see my own sister
Marry one. Even if she
Loved him, think of the children.
Their art is interesting,
But certainly barbarous.
I'm sure, if given a chance,
They'd kill us all in our beds.
And you must admit, they smell.

The News You Don't Get at Home

Luis J. Rodríguez

The news you don't get at home
is in the dangling flesh of peasants and workers,
in the silenced tongues of poets and journalists,
in the machine-gunned remains of women and children.

The news you don't get at home
is molded, packaged, abbreviated,
synthesized, and castrated,
through the phone lines,
from the bleeding pens of eyeless stooges
who went to all the fine schools,
worked on all the fine newspapers,
who covered the great wars
("Hey, is this Lebanon or El Salvador?")
who wired in the fabrications to fit the ignorance,
who sat in small, dingy hotels with great scotch
and claimed to be truthsayers.

Somehow these "journalists" failed to see
the election fraud; the names of the dead
resurrected on election rosters
(and they say there are no miracles in this world!).
They failed to see the trucked-in thugs
from out of town
and the death threats carved on the inside
of a woman's thigh.

The news you don't get at home
is in the withered eye sockets
of emaciated faces, seeking food,
seeking redress, seeking emancipation—
oh, such a word!
It rarely makes the sweaty copy
of these "objective observers,"
these TV-bred, English 101-graduates
who know where the semicolons go
but who couldn't find the heart of humanity
in an outstretched hand.

Wise I

Amiri Baraka

WHYS (Nobody Knows
The Trouble I Seen)
Trad.

If you ever find
yourself, some where
lost and surrounded
by enemies
who won't let you
speak in your own language
who destroy your statues
& instruments, who ban
you omm bomm ba boom
then you are in trouble
deep trouble
they ban your
own boom ba boom
you in deep deep
trouble

humph!

probably take you several hundred years
to get
out!

Poem in the American Manner

Dorothy Parker

I dunno yer highfalutin' words, but here's th' way it seems
When I'm peekin' out th' winder o' my little House o Dreams;
I've been lookin' 'roun' this big ol' world, as bizzy as a hive,
An' I want t' tell ye, neighbor mine, it's good t' be alive.
I've ben settin' here, a-thinkin' hard, an' say, it seems t' me
That this big ol' world is jest about as good as it kin be,
With its starvin' little babies, an' its battles, an' its strikes,
An' its profiteers, an' hold-up men—th' dawggone little tykes!
An' its hungry men that fought fer us, that nobody employs.
An' I think, "Why, shucks, we're jest a lot o' grown-up little boys!"
An' I settle back, an' light my pipe, an' reach fer Mother's hand,
An' I wouldn't swap my peace o' mind fer nothin' in the land;
Fer this world uv ours, that jest was made fer folks like me an' you
Is a purty good ol' place t' live—say, neighbor, ain't it true?

Possessor's Pity

George Abbe

The owner of this city has been more than kind
and tender in his wishes for us all.
I saw him pasting bank notes on the blind,
hiding the dead-from-hunger behind a wall.

I saw a street car with bumpers of velour
run over frightened people most considerately:
the bones broke softly, and a velvet sewer
received the bodies—buried without fee.

I saw the needy naked in department stores
placed in a bronze globe dewy with perfume
which whirled them with subdued and pleasant roar
till they forgot their need of board and room.

I saw the starving sorrowed-for and loved
by a long procession of the richly clad
who touched thin, dying bodies with their gloves,
asked for a priest, slowly removed their hats.

The factory owner, compassionate and able,
saw that the hand torn by the new machine
was wrapped in linen napkins from his table,
a note sent to the workman's wife who grieved.

The owner of these owners, wherever he was,
could not be seen, but he was more than good:
on the prone body of each unemployed
he placed a vase of flowers to serve as food.

Liberty Needs Glasses

Tupac Shakur

excuse me but Lady Liberty needs glasses
And so does Mrs. Justice by her side
Both the broads R blind as bats
Stumbling thru the system
Justice bumped into Mutulu and
Trippin' on Geronimo Pratt
But stepped right over Oliver
And his crooked partner Ronnie
Justice stubbed her Big Toe on Mandela
And liberty was misquoted by the Indians
slavery was a learning phase
Forgotten without a verdict
while Justice is on a rampage
4 endangered surviving Black males
I mean really if anyone really valued life
and cared about the masses
They'd take 'em both 2 Pen Optical
and get 2 pairs of glasses

we are all getting burned

Misery
Langston Hughes

*Misery is when you heard
on the radio that the neighborhood
you live in is a slum but
you always thought it was home.*

Mexico Is Sinking

Guillermo Gómez-Peña

Mexico is sinking
California is on Fire
& we all are getting burned
aren't we?
But what if suddenly the continent turned upside down?
what if the U.S. was Mexico?
what if 200,000 Anglo-Saxicans
were to cross the border each month
to work as gardeners, waiters,
3rd chair musicians, movie extras,
bouncers, babysitters, chauffeurs,
syndicated cartoons, feather-weight boxers, fruit-pickers, &
anonymous poets?
what if they were called waspanos,
waspitos, wasperos or waspbacks?
what if we were the top dogs?
what if literature was life, eh?
what if yo were you
& tú fueras I, Mister?

Columbus Day

Jimmie Durham

In school I was taught the names
Columbus, Cortez, and Pizarro and
A dozen other filthy murderers.
A bloodline all the way to General Miles,
Daniel Boone and General Eisenhower.

No one mentioned the names
Of even a few of the victims.
But don't you remember Chaske, whose spine
Was crushed so quickly by Mr. Pizzaro's boot?
What words did he cry into the dust?

What was the familiar name
Of that young girl who danced so gracefully
That everyone in the village sang with her—
Before Cortez' sword hacked off her arms
As she protested the burning of her sweetheart?

That young man's name was Many Deeds,
And he had been a leader of a band of fighters
Called the Redstick Hummingbirds, who slowed
The march of Cortez' army with only a few
Spears and stones which now lay still
In the mountains and remember.

Greenrock Woman was the name
Of that old lady who walked right up
And spat in Columbus' face. We
Must remember that, and remember
Laughing Otter the Taino, who tried to stop
Columbus and who was taken away as a slave.
We never saw him again.

In school I learned of heroic discoveries
Made by liars and crooks. The courage
Of millions of sweet and true people
Was not commemorated.

Let us then declare a holiday
For ourselves, and make a parade that begins
With Columbus' victims and continues
Even to our grandchildren who will be named
In their honor.
Because isn't it true that even the summer
Grass here in this land whispers those names,
And every creek has accepted the responsibility
Of singing those names? And nothing can stop
The wind from howling those names around
The corners of the school.

Why else would the birds sing
So much sweeter here than in other lands?

Points of View

Ishmael Reed

The pioneers and the indians
disagree about a lot of things
for example, the pioneer says that
when you meet a bear in the woods
you should yell at him and if that
doesn't work, you should fell him
The indians say that you should
whisper to him softly and call him by
loving nicknames
No one's bothered to ask the bear
what he thinks

The Handicapped

Philip Dacey

1
The missing legs
of the amputee
are away somewhere
winning a secret race.

2
The blind man has always stood
before an enormous blackboard,
waiting for the first
scrawl of light,
that fine
dusty chalk.

3
Here
the repetitions of the stutterer,
there
the flickering of the stars.

4
Master of illusion,
the paralytic alone moves.
All else is still.

5
At Creation,
God told the deaf,
"Only you will hear
the song of the stone."

6
Dare not ask
what the dumb
have been told to keep secret.

7
When the epileptic
falls in a fit,
he is ascending
to the heaven of earth.

Bilingual Christmas
Do you hear what I hear?
Pat Mora

Buenos días and *hasta luego*
in boardrooms and strategy sessions.
Where are your grateful holiday smiles,
bilinguals? I've given you a voice,
let you in
to hear old friends tell old jokes.
Stop flinching. Drink eggnog. Hum along.

> Not carols we hear
> whimpering
> children too cold
> to sing
> on Christmas eve.

> Do you see what I see

adding a dash of color
to conferences and corporate parties
one per panel or office
slight south-of-the-border seasoning
feliz navidad and *próspero año nuevo,* right?
Relax. Eat rum balls. Watch the snow.

> Not twinkling lights
> we see but
> searchlights
> seeking illegal aliens
> outside our thick windows.

Man in Space

Billy Collins

All you have to do is listen to the way a man
sometimes talks to his wife at a table of people
and notice how intent he is on making his point
even though her lower lip is beginning to quiver,

and you will know why the women in science
fiction movies who inhabit a planet of their own
are not pictured making a salad or reading a magazine
when the men from earth arrive in their rocket,

why they are always standing in a semicircle
with their arms folded, their bare legs set apart,
their breasts protected by hard metal disks.

Indian Movie, New Jersey

Chitra Banerjee Divakaruni

Not like the white filmstars, all rib
and gaunt cheekbone, the Indian sex-goddess
smiles plumply from behind a flowery branch.
Below her brief red skirt, her thighs
are solid and redeeming
as tree trunks. She swings her hips
and the men viewers whistle. The lover-hero
dances in to a song, his lip sync
a little off, but no matter, we
know the words already and sing along.
It is safe here, the day
golden and cool so no one sweats,
roses on every bush and the Dal Lake
clean again.
   The sex-goddess switches
to thickened English to emphasize
a joke. We laugh and clap. Here
we need not be embarrassed
by mispronounced phrases
dropping like hot lead into foreign ears.
The flickering movie light
wipes from our faces years of America,
sons who want mohawks and refuse
to run the family store, daughters who date
on the sly.
   When at the end the hero
dies for his friend who also
loves the sex-goddess and now can marry her,
we weep, understanding. Even the men
clear their throats to say, "What *qurbani!*
What *dosti!*" After, we mill around,
unwilling to leave, exchange greetings
and good news: a new gold chain, a trip
to India. We do not speak

of motel raids, cancelled permits, stones
thrown through glass windows, daughters and sons
raped by Dotbusters.
      In this dim foyer
we can pull around us the faint comforting smell
of incense and *pakoras*, can arrange
our children's marriages with hometown boys and girls,
open a franchise, win a million
in the mail. We can retire in India,
a yellow two storied house
with wrought-iron gates, our own
Ambassador car. Or at least
move to a rich white suburb, Summerfield
or Fort Lee, with neighbors that will
talk to us. Here while the film songs still echo
in the corridors and restrooms, we can trust
in movie truths: sacrifice, success, love and luck,
the America that was supposed to be.

Note
qurbani: sacrifice
dosti: friendship
Dotbusters: anti-Indian gangs

The Geography of Poetry
for ntozake shange
Assotto Saint

ntozake shange
i looked you up
among the poets at barnes & noble
but i didn't find you

walt was there amidst leaves of grass
anne gazed down
her glazed eyes dreamt of rowing mercy
erica posed in her latest erotica
even rod took much space
i searched among ghosts
& those alive
still
i couldn't find you

i asked the clerk
if he had kept you tied down in boxes
or does he use your books as dart boards
he smirked then shouted "she's in the black section
in the back"
even literature has its ghettos

stacked amongst langston, nikki, & countee
maya who looked mad
the blues had her bad
zake tell me
did you demand to be segregated
"does color modify poetry"
i asked the manager

he patted me on my head
whispered
"it's always been this way"

Invisibility Poem: Lesbian

Ilze Mueller

There's quite enough to
identify her
should you have forgotten
her name:
That woman who lives in
who teaches
who speaks
who looks like
who writes about
the one who knows
the one who made
the one who loves to
who likes to wear
whose daughter
who used to be
wasn't she married to
didn't she once spend some time
Every known thing about her
is like a smell
reassuring, familiar
"She is like us"
"We are like her"
No need to watch
suspiciously
when she walks by.
Not as familiar perhaps
the things she keeps
invisible:
The woman with whom
the circle of friends that she
the way she feels when
the thoughts she doesn't
the fear that keeps her from
the times she imagines
the price she pays for

La Migra

Pat Mora

1
Let's play La Migra.
I'll be the Border Patrol.
You be the Mexican maid.
I get the badge and sunglasses.
You can hide and run,
but you can't get away
because I have a jeep.
I can take you wherever
I want, but don't ask
questions because
I don't speak Spanish.
I can touch you wherever
I want but don't complain
too much because I've got
boots and kick—if I have to,
and I have handcuffs.
Oh, and a gun.
Get ready, get set, run.

2
Let's play La Migra.
You be the Border Patrol.
I'll be the Mexican woman.
Your jeep has a flat,
and you have been spotted
by the sun.
All you have is heavy: hat,
glasses, badge, shoes, gun.
I know this desert,
where to rest,
where to drink.
Oh, I am not alone.
You hear us singing
and laughing with the wind,
Agua dulce brota aquí, aquí, aquí,
but since you can't speak Spanish,
you do not understand.
Get ready.

Picasso
Ellyn Maybe

I found a year that likes my body
    1921
girl sitting on a rock
Picasso painted a woman
with my thighs

walking around the museum
it hit me how Rubenesque
is not just some word
for someone who likes corned beef

there I was
naked on the edge of something
overlooking water
or was it salt

it was weird
nobody was screaming fat chick at the frame
nobody was making grieving sounds
but the girl in the painting looked sad

as though she knew
new ears were smudging
a forced liposuction
with rough acrylic

the caption said
girl sitting on rock

not woman who uses food to help cope
for the lack of empathy in her sphere

not the gyms are closed and there are
better muscles to develop

not girl one calorie away
from suicide

just flesh on a rock

her eyes dripping
question marks onto
girl looking into a mirror

the vibrancy
the need to chew the ice cubism
till the teeth bleed
the colors so deep
they look wet

the museum guards
watch me tentatively
I lean into the paintings
I veer to the outside
to find out what Picasso
called each work

I like titles
their vocabulary of oil
the girl on the rock
whispered to me

go girl

I love museums
call me old fashioned
but I like face to face
conversations.

Sure You Can Ask Me A Personal Question

Diane Burns

How do you do?
    No, I am not Chinese.
No, not Spanish.
    No, I am American Indi-uh, Native American.
No, not from India.
    No, not Apache.
No, not Navajo.
    No, not Sioux.
No, we are not extinct.
    Yes, Indian.
Oh?
    So that's where you got those high cheekbones.
Your great grandmother, huh?
    An Indian Princess, huh?
Hair down to there?
    Let me guess. Cherokee?
Oh, so you've had an Indian friend?
    That close?
Oh, so you've had an Indian lover?
    That tight?
Oh, so you've had an Indian servant?
    That much?
Yeah, it was awful what you guys did to us.
    It's real decent of you to apologize.
No, I don't know where you can get peyote.
    No, I don't know where you can get Navajo rugs real cheap.
No, I didn't make this. I bought it at Bloomingdales.
    Thank you. I like your hair too.

I don't know if anyone knows whether or not Cher is really Indian.
No, I didn't make it rain tonight.
Yeah. Uh-huh. Spirituality.
Uh-huh. Yeah. Spirituality. Uh-huh. Mother
Earth. Yeah. Uh'huh. Uh-huh. Spirituality.
No, I didn't major in archery.
Yeah, a lot of us drink too much.
Some of us can't drink enough.
This ain't no stoic look.
This is my face.

L.A. Prayer
April 1992

Francisco X. Alarcón

something   the more
was wrong   we run
when buses   the more
didn't come   we burn

streets   o god
were   show us
no longer   the way
streets   lead us

how easy   spare us
hands   from ever
became   turning into
weapons   walking

blows   matches
gunfire   amidst
rupturing   so much
the night   gasoline

giving secrets away

Other People's Lives
Alice Mishkin

You have to see
Other people's lives
Before you recognize
Your own.

Windshield

Alicia Ostriker

You are supposed to roll your windows up
Driving through certain neighborhoods
Because they are waiting for you at the intersections,
For you or anyone,
Where cars go bumper to bumper,
Flirtatious shadows, wanting to clean your windshield,
Perhaps, or to shoot you, the way they shot my friend
The talkative flutist, lost on Detroit's avenues,
Through his open old Ford window.
Got him in the cheek and shoulder,
No reason. He was just busy talking, and the summer
Evening was stifling.
Up at the red light now, they are doing their crisp dance
With their rags and squeegees
Around a helpless Subaru.
Watch it, mister—
A warrior strut, a cottonmouth snap to remind you
Of the wet odor of rural underbrush,
A little twirl, a little
Hustle on oily cobblestones.
When one of them advances on you, yellow eyes
And shining teeth, denim slung
Low on a wasted pelvis, you can feel
In your bones the awful
Cruelty of his life,
Nothing to lose—
As looking at you sitting behind windowglass
Just at the moment you resist the urge
Your foot has, to jam on the gas,
He sees that blank expression flattening
Your face like a heavy drug, and he
Can feel the cruelty
Of yours, man, right in his bones.

St. Peter Claver

Toi Derricotte

Every town with black Catholics has a St. Peter Claver's.
My first was nursery school.
Miss Maturin made us fold our towels in a regulation square and nap
    on army cots.
No mother questioned; no child sassed.
In blue pleated skirts, pants, and white shirts,
we stood in line to use the open toilets
and conserved light by walking in darkness.
Unsmiling, mostly light-skinned, we were the children of the middle
    class, preparing to take our parents' places in a world that would
    demand we fold our hands and wait.
They said it was good for us, the bowl of soup, its pasty whiteness;
I learned to swallow and distrust my senses.

On holy cards St. Peter's face is olive-toned, his hair near kinky;
I thought he was one of us who pass between the rich and poor, the
    light and dark.
Now I read he was "a Spanish Jesuit priest who labored for the salvation
    of the African Negroes and the abolition of the slave trade."
I was tricked again, robbed of my patron,
and left with a debt to another white man.

Being a Good *Americani*

Fawaz Turki

Last Sunday was a fine day
for me to be a good *Americani*.
I painted the kitchen table
and talked to my next door neighbor
while he washed his car.
In between all of that,
I scolded my son for playing
with his genitals,
ate french fries,
fought with my wife
and talked to her mother long distance.
Before it got dark
I hopped in the car
and bought sliced salami,
toilet paper
and a six pack of beer
at 7-Eleven.
At the store
I conversed with the customers
about who shot JR.
The clerk joined in the conversation
and offered a learned
conjecture on who the murderer was.
Soon the sun had set
on Arlington, Virginia,
where I have lived with
my American family for a decade,
trying,
desperately,
to be a good *Americani*.

I watched TV for three hours
and then went to bed.
I thought about our dog
who had died recently.
I would have taken him for a walk
around this time.
My wife hoped I did not mind
that she was not in the mood tonight.
I said honey I don't mind either.
So she combed her blond hair
and I read *Time* magazine.
I had my life
figured out cold for me.
Only from time to time
I wake up in the middle of the night,
or maybe somewhere when the night
is just fading into day,
when the moment
is neither here nor there,
which is a safe time to think
about Palestine and olive trees,
and I pity myself
and the place I came from.

Look Back
Gogisgi

I listen to this
86 year old
whiteman chuckle about
years ago when he
and the other boys
dug up Seminole
graves and used the skulls
for target practice.

I listen, say
nothing, leave the room
quietly. I am
supposed to respect
this man who is
my wife's father.

I listen, knowing
this old man who
is so kind to
his family, who
fears so much but
respects nothing,
will soon be gone.

Still listening,
knowing something
is going to happen,
something bad
is going to happen,
something bad
is going to keep on
happening.

Award
[A Gold Watch to the FBI Man
(who has followed me) for 25 Years.]

Ray Durem

Well, old spy
looks like I
led you down some pretty blind alleys,
took you on several trips to Mexico,
fishing in the high Sierras,
jazz at the Philharmonic.
You've watched me all your life,
I've clothed your wife,
put your two sons through college.
what good has it done?
sun keeps rising every morning.
Ever see me buy an Assistant President?
or close a school?
or lend money to Somoza?
I bought some after-hours whiskey in L.A.
but the Chief got his pay.
I ain't killed no Koreans,
or fourteen-year-old boys in Mississippi
neither did I bomb Guatemala,
or lend guns to shoot Algerians.
I admit I took a Negro child
to a white rest room in Texas,
but she was my daughter, only three,
and she had to pee,
and I just didn't know what to do,
would you?
see, I'm so light, it don't seem right
to go to the colored rest room;
my daughter's brown, and folks frown on that in Texas,
I just don't know how to go to the bathroom in the free world!

Now, old FBI man,
you've done the best you can,
you lost me a few jobs,
scared a couple landlords,
You got me struggling for that bread,
but I ain't dead.
and before it's all through,
I may be following you!

In Response to Executive Order 9066: All Americans of Japanese Descent Must Report to Relocation Centers

Dwight Okita

Dear Sirs:
Of course I'll come. I've packed my galoshes
and three packets of tomato seeds. Denise calls them
love apples. My father says where we're going
they won't grow.

I am a fourteen-year-old girl with bad spelling
and a messy room. If it helps any, I will tell you
I have always felt funny using chopsticks
and my favorite food is hot dogs.
My best friend is a white girl named Denise –
we look at boys together. She sat in front of me
all through grade school because of our names:
O'Connor, Ozawa. I know the back of Denise's head very well.

I tell her she's going bald. She tells me I copy on tests.
We're best friends.

I saw Denise today in Geography class.
She was sitting on the other side of the room.
"You're trying to start a war," she said, "giving secrets
away to the Enemy, Why can't you keep your big
mouth shut?"

I didn't know what to say.
I gave her a packet of tomato seeds
and asked her to plant them for me, told her
when the first tomato ripened
she'd miss me.

Harlem Hopscotch

Maya Angelou

One foot down, then hop! It's hot.
  Good things for the ones that's got.
Another jump, now to the left.
  Everybody for hisself.

In the air, now both feet down.
  Since you black, don't stick around.
Food is gone, the rent is due,
  Curse and cry and then jump two.

All the people out of work,
  Hold for three, then twist and jerk.
Cross the line, they count you out.
  That's what hopping's all about.

Both feet flat, the game is done.
They think I lost. I think I won.

Please Fire Me

Deborah Garrison

Here comes another alpha male,
and all the other alphas
are snorting and pawing,
kicking up puffs of acrid dust

while the silly little hens
clatter back and forth
on quivering claws and raise
a titter about the fuss.

Here comes another alpha male—
a man's man, a dealmaker,
holds tanks of liquor,
charms them pantsless at lunch:

I've never been sicker.
Do I have to stare into his eyes
and sympathize? If I want my job
I do. Well I think I'm through

with the working world,
through with warming eggs
and being Zenlike in my detachment
from all things Ego.

I'd like to go
somewhere else entirely,
and I don't mean
Europe.

The Legend

Garrett Hongo

In Chicago, it is snowing softly
and a man has just done his wash for the week.
He steps into the twilight of early evening,
carrying a wrinkled shopping bag
full of neatly folded clothes,
and, for a moment, enjoys
the feel of warm laundry and crinkled paper,
flannellike against his gloveless hands.
There's a Rembrandt glow on his face,
a triangle of orange in the hollow of his cheek
as a last flash of sunset
blazes the storefronts and lit windows of the street.

He is Asian, Thai or Vietnamese,
and very skinny, dressed as one of the poor
in rumpled suit pants and a plaid mackinaw,
dingy and too large.
He negotiates the slick of ice
on the sidewalk by his car,
opens the Fairlane's back door,
leans to place the laundry in,
and turns, for an instant,
toward the flurry of footsteps
and cries of pedestrians
as a boy — that's all he was —
backs from the corner package store
shooting a pistol, firing it,
once, at the dumbfounded man
who falls forward,
grabbing at his chest.

A few sounds escape from his mouth,
a babbling no one understands
as people surround him
bewildered at his speech.
The noises he makes are nothing to them.
The boy has gone, lost
in the light array of foot traffic
dappling the snow with fresh prints.

Tonight, I read about Descartes'
grand courage to doubt everything
except his own miraculous existence
and I feel so distinct
from the wounded man lying on the concrete
I am ashamed.

Let the night sky cover him as he dies.
Let the weaver girl cross the bridge of heaven
and take up his cold hands.

In memory of Jay Kashiwamura

White Lies

Natasha Trethewey

The lies I could tell,
when I was growing up
light-bright, near-white,
high-yellow, red-boned
in a black place,
were just white lies.

I could easily tell the white folks
that we lived uptown,
not in that pink and green
shanty-fied shotgun section
along the tracks. I could act
like my homemade dresses
came straight out the window
of Maison Blanche. I could even
keep quiet, quiet as kept,
like the time a white girl said
(squeezing my hand), *Now*
we have three of us in this class.

But I paid for it every time
Mama found out.
She laid her hands on me,
then washed out my mouth
with Ivory soap. *This*
is to purify, she said,
and cleanse your lying tongue.
Believing her, I swallowed suds
thinking they'd work
from the inside out.

This is a poem to my son Peter

Peter Meinke

this is a poem to my son Peter
whom I have hurt a thousand times
whose large and vulnerable eyes
have glazed in pain at my ragings
thin wrists and fingers hung
boneless in despair, pale freckled back
bent in defeat, pillow soaked
by my failure to understand.
I have scarred through weakness
and impatience your frail confidence forever
because when I needed to strike
you were there to be hurt and because
I thought you knew
you were beautiful and fair
your bright eyes and hair
but now I see that no one knows that
about himself, but must be told
and retold until it takes hold
because I think anything can be killed
after a while, especially beauty
so I write this for life, for love, for
you, my oldest son Peter, age 10,
going on 11.

Warning

Mitsuye Yamada

The voice of my father came to me
from a corner of his cell
(marked Dangerous Enemy Alien)

Do not sign your legal name
to anything not
on petitions for any cause
in the street
at meetings or rallies
not on receipts for orders,
special deliveries or C.O.D.s

I was my father's daughter
I had followed his advice assiduously
never left my thumbprints anywhere
never gave my stamp of approval
to anything
never cast my soulprint in cement
never raised my voice on billboards
and one day disappeared anyway
behind barbed wires.
They put up a sign on buildings
telephone poles and store fronts:
For all persons who never left a mark.

"My silences had not protected me."*

*Audre Lorde, MLA convention, Chicago, 1977

Outwitted

Edwin Markham

He drew a circle that shut me out —
Heretic, a rebel, a thing to flout.
But Love and I had the wit to win:
We drew a circle that took him in!

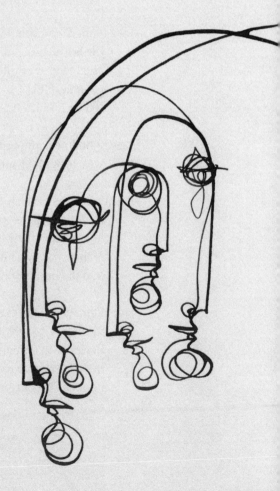

My Great-Grandfather's Slaves

Wendell Berry

Deep in the back ways of my mind I see them
    going in the long days
    over the same fields that I have gone
    long days over.

I see the sun passing and burning high
    over that land from their day
    until mine, their shadows
    having risen and consumed them.

I see them obeying and watching
    the bearded tall man whose voice
    and blood are mine, whose countenance
    in stone at his grave my own resembles,
    whose blindness is my brand.

I see them kneel and pray to the white God
    who buys their souls with Heaven.

I see them approach, quiet
    in the merchandise of their flesh,
    to put down their burdens
    of firewood and hemp and tobacco
    into the minds of my kinsmen.

I see them moving in the rooms of my history,
    the day of my birth entering
    the horizon emptied of their days,
    their purchased lives taken back
    into the dust of birthright.

I see them borne, shadow within shadow,
    shroud within shroud, through all nights
    from their lives to mine, long beyond
    reparation or given liberty
    or any straightness.

I see them go in the bonds of my blood
    through all the time of their bodies.

I have seen that freedom cannot be taken
    from one man and given to another,
    and cannot be taken and kept.

I know that freedom can only be given,
    and is the gift to the giver
    from the one who receives.

I am owned by the blood of all of them
    who ever were owned by my blood.
    We cannot be free of each other.

Riding the D-Train

Enid Dame

Notice the rooftops,
the wormeaten Brooklyn buildings.
Houses crawl by,
each with its private legend.
In one, a mother
is punishing her child
slowly, with great enjoyment.
In one, a daughter
is writing a novel
she can't show to anyone.

Notice your fellow riders:
the Asian girl chewing a toothpick,
the boy drawing trees on his hand,
the man in a business suit
whose shoes don't match.

Everything is important:
that thin girl, for instance,
in flowered dress, golden high heels.
How did her eyes get scarred?
Why is that old man crying?
Why does that woman carry
a cat in her pocketbook?

Don't underestimate
any of it.

Anything you don't see
will come back to haunt you.

jap
Lee Herrick

windshield to windshield
we are parked
like matadors,
pumping gas at the am pm.
It is a normal afternoon in the valley
like all afternoons in the valley,
split between modern duty
and the desire of something better.

We are in the same world.
I pull in and
face you, but
my sunglasses shield my almond
eyes, and what you don't realize
is that I see you.
I see you
in your red anger,
your believed anonymity
your life boiling you to this ugly place,
where, in the pain of inarticulacy,
your vomit words,
like swords,
hurled at me:

god   damn   jap

I look down at my chest
my almond eyes open wide
breath sputtering
blood dripping.
I pull it from just beside my heart
and I still stand.

This is where racism begins
in the throat
at the station
in the heart of valley afternoons.

I hold your bloody words,
walking to you slowly
with sword in hand.
I have been here before, have you?
I can show you knife wounds
on my chest
like constellations

I approach you and you fear
something, my difference
I imagine
Instead of thrusting this bloody sword
back into you and killing us both off
slowly, I whisper to you:

I am not god
I am not damned
and I am not Japanese

I drop the sword and feel
my chest, stronger
and I imagine a space
with no swords
and
no constellations

Admission of Failure

Phyllis Koestenbaum

The hostess seats a girl and a young man in a short-sleeve
sport shirt with one arm missing below the shoulder. I'm at
the next table with my husband and son, Andy's Barbeque
Restaurant, an early evening in July, chewing a boneless
rib eye, gulping a dark beer ordered from the cocktail
waitress, a nervous woman almost over the hill, whose high
heel sandals click back and forth from the bar to the
dining room joined to the bar by an open arch. A tall heavy
cook in white hat is brushing sauce on the chicken and
spareribs rotating slowly on a squeaking spit. Baked
potatoes heat on the oven floor. The young man is eating
salad with his one hand. He and his girl are on a date. He
has a forties' movie face, early Van Johnson before the
motorcycle accident scarred his forehead. He lost the arm
recently. Hard as it is, it could be worse. I would even
exchange places with him if I could. *I want to exchange*
places with the young armless man in the barbeque
restaurant. He would sit at my table and I would sit at
his. After dinner I would go in his car and he would go in
mine. I would live in his house and work at his job and he
would live in my house and do what I do. I would be him
dressing and undressing and he would be me dressing and
undressing. Our bill comes. My husband leaves the tip on
the tray; we take toothpicks and mints and walk through the
dark workingmen's bar out to the parking lot still lit by
the sky though the streetlights have come on as they do
automatically at the same time each night. We drive our
son, home for the summer, back to his job at the bookstore.
As old Italians and Jews say of sons from five to fifty,
he's a good boy. I have worked on this paragraph for more
than two years.

Anglo-Saxon Protestant Heterosexual Men

Wendell Berry

Come, dear brothers,
let us cheerfully acknowledge
that we are the last hope of the world,
for we have no excuses,
nobody to blame but ourselves.
Who is going to sit at our feet
and listen while we bewail
our historical sufferings? Who
will ever believe that we also
have wept in the night
with repressed longing to become
our real selves? Who will
stand forth and proclaim
that we have virtues and talents
peculiar to our category? Nobody,
and that is good. For here we are
at last with our real selves
in the real world. Therefore,
let us quiet our hearts, my brothers,
and settle down for a change
to picking up after ourselves
and a few centuries of honest work.

Sympathy

Paul Laurence Dunbar

I know what the caged bird feels, alas!
 When the sun is bright on the upland slopes;
When the wind stirs soft through the spring grass,
And the river flows like a stream of glass;
 When the first bird sings and the first bud opes,
And the faint perfume from its chalice steals –
I know what the caged bird feels!

I know why the caged bird beats his wing
 Till its blood is red on the cruel bars;
For he must fly back to his perch and cling
When he fain would be on the bough a-swing;
 And a pain still throbs in the old, old scars
And they pulse again with a keener sting –
I know why he beats his wing!

I know why the caged bird sings, ah me,
 When his wing is bruised and his bosom sore, –
When he beats his bars and he would be free;
It is not a carol of joy or glee,
 But a prayer that he sends from his heart's deep core,
But a plea, that upward to Heaven he flings –
I know why the caged bird sings!

A Ritual to Read to Each Other
William Stafford

If you don't know the kind of person I am
and I don't know the kind of person you are
a pattern that others made may prevail in the
     world
and following the wrong god home we may miss
     our star.

For there is many a small betrayal in the mind,
a shrug that lets the fragile sequence break
sending with shouts the horrible errors of
     childhood
storming out to play through the broken dike.

And as elephants parade holding each
     elephant's tail,
but if one wanders the circus won't find the
     park,
I call it cruel and maybe the root of all cruelty
to know what occurs but not recognize the fact.

And so I appeal to a voice, to something
     shadowy,
a remote important region in all who talk:
though we could fool each other, we should
     consider –
lest the parade of our mutual life get lost in the
     dark.

For it is important that awake people be awake,
or a breaking line may discourage them back to
     sleep;
the signals we give – yes or no, or maybe –
should be clear: the darkness around us is deep.

Failing in the Presence of Ants

Gary Soto

We live to some purpose, daughter.
Across the park, among
The trees that give the eye
Something to do, let's spread
A blanket on the ground
And examine the ants, loose
Thread to an old coat.
Perhaps they are more human than we are.
They live for the female,
Rescue their hurt, and fall earthward
For their small cause. And
Us? We live for our bellies,
The big O of our mouths.
Give me, give me, they say,
And many people, whole countries,
May go under because we desire TV
And chilled drinks, clothes
That hang well on our bodies –
Desire sofas and angled lamps,
Hair the sea may envy
On a slow day.
It is hurtful to sweep
Ants into a frenzy, blow
Chemicals into their eyes –
Those austere marchers who will lift
Their heads to rumor – seed,
Wafer of leaf, dropped apple –
And start off, over this
And that, between sloppy feet
And staggered chairs, for no
Purpose other than it might be good.

Sunrise

Mary Oliver

You can
die for it —
an idea,
or the world. People

have done so,
brilliantly,
letting
their small bodies be bound

to the stake,
creating
an unforgettable
fury of light. But

this morning,
climbing the familiar hills
in the familiar
fabric of dawn, I thought

of China,
and India
and Europe, and I thought
how the sun

blazes
for everyone just
so joyfully
as it rises

under the lashes
of my own eyes, and I thought
I am so many!
What is my name?

What is the name
of the deep breath I would take
over and over
for all of us? Call it

whatever you want, it is
happiness, it is another one
of the ways to enter
fire.

the next thing to happen

The Greater Thing
Edwin Markham

Great is it to believe the dream
When we stand in youth by the starry stream;
But a greater thing is to fight life through
And say at the end, "The dream was true."

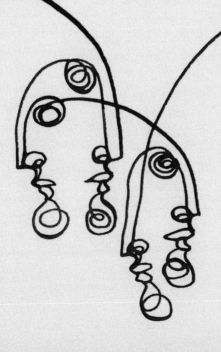

Piece by Piece

Luis J. Rodriguez

Piece by piece
They tear at you:
Peeling away layers of being,
Lying about who you are,
Speaking for your dreams.

In the squalor of their eyes
You are an outlaw.
Dressing you in a jacket of lies
– tailor made in steel –
You fit their perfect picture.

Take it off!
Make your own mantle.
Question the interrogators.
Eyeball the death in their gaze.
Say you won't succumb.
Say you won't believe them
When they rename you.
Say you won't accept their codes,
Their colors, their putrid morals.

Here you have a way.
Here you can sing victory.
Here you are not a conquered race
Perpetual victim –
The sullen face in a thunderstorm.

Hands/mind, they are carving out
A sanctuary.
Use these weapons against them.
Use your given gifts –
They are not stone.

Freedom of Expression
William Stafford

My feet wait there listening, and when
they dislike what happens they begin
to press on the floor. They know when
it is time to walk out on a program. Pretty soon
they are moving, and as the program fades
you can hear the sound of my feet on gravel.

If you have feet with standards, you too
may be reminded – you need not
accept what's given. You gamblers,
pimps, braggarts, oppressive people: –
"Not here," my feet are saying, "no thanks;
let me out of this." And I'm gone.

Marked

Carmen Tafolla

Never write with pencil,
m'ija.
It is for those
who would
erase.
Make your mark proud
      and open,
Brave,
      beauty folded into
  its imperfection,
Like a piece of turquoise
    marked.

Never write
with pencil,
m'ija.

Write with ink
    or mud,
or berries grown in
gardens never owned,
    or, sometimes,
      if necessary,
      blood.

Prayer

Louis Untermeyer

God, though this life is but a wraith,
    Although we know not what we use,
Although we grope with little faith,
    Give me the heart to fight – and lose.

Ever insurgent let me be,
    Make me more daring than devout;
From sleek contentment keep me free,
    And fill me with a buoyant doubt.

Open my eyes to visions girt
    With beauty, and with wonder lit –
But let me always see the dirt,
    And all that spawn and die in it.

Open my ears to music; let
    Me thrill with Spring's first flutes and drums –
But never let me dare forget
    The bitter ballads of the slums.

From compromise and things half-done,
    Keep me, with stern and stubborn pride;
And when, at last, the fight is won,
    God, keep me still unsatisfied.

The Last Word

Amina Baraka

i'd rather my fist be made of steel
than my heel made of iron
i'd rather water the earth with my tears
than lose feeling
i'd rather walk
than ride the backs of workers
i'd rather die fighting
than live slaving
i'd rather be criticized for protest poetry
than write lines indifferent to my people's lives
leave me to my "propaganda"
let my songs call for Freedom
turn down my manuscripts
poem after poem
tell me i'm repetitious
the word oppression is used too much
i'd rather complain
than say nothing at all
i hope my last words
call for revolution
i'd rather my pen
be at least as mighty as the sword

Perhaps the World Ends Here
Joy Harjo

The world begins at a kitchen table. No matter what, we must eat
to live.

The gifts of earth are brought and prepared, set on the table. So it
has been since creation, and it will go on.

We chase chickens or dogs away from it. Babies teethe at the corners.
They scrape their knees under it.

It is here that children are given instructions on what it means to be
human. We make men at it, we make women.

At this table we gossip, recall enemies and the ghosts of lovers.

Our dreams drink coffee with us as they put their arms around our
children. They laugh with us at our poor falling-down selves and as
we put ourselves back together once again at the table.

This table has been a house in the rain, an umbrella in the sun.

Wars have begun and ended at this table. It is a place to hide in the
shadow of terror. A place to celebrate the terrible victory.

We have given birth on this table, and have prepared our parents for burial here.

At this table we sing with joy, with sorrow. We pray of suffering
and remorse. We give thanks.

Perhaps the world will end at the kitchen table, while we are laughing and
crying, eating of the last sweet bite.

Being a Person
William Stafford

Be a person here. Stand by the river, invoke
the owls. Invoke winter, then spring.
Let any season that wants to come here make its own
call. After that sound goes away, wait.

A slow bubble rises through the earth
and begins to include sky, stars, all space,
even the outracing, expanding thought.
Come back and hear the little sound again.

Suddenly this dream you are having matches
everyone's dream, and the result is the world.
If a different call came there wouldn't be any
world, or you, or the river, or the owls calling.

How you stand here is important. How you
listen for the next thing to happen. How you breathe.

With all thy wide geographies, manifold, different, distant,
Rounding by thee in One – one common orbic language,
One common indivisible destiny and Union.

Walt Whitman, Leaves of Grass

Biographical Notes*

*Every bit of information used in the writing of the Biographical Notes was found online and not verified by authenticated sources nor attributed to original authors. Therefore, consider it to be suspicious and not to be used without further research, verification, and attribution to the original source once found. While undeniably fascinating, please note that these notes are certifiably uncertified.

George Bancroft Abbe "Possessor's Pity" (1911, Somers, CT, – 1989) Sylvia Plath wrote in her journal that Abbe had a sad, poor boyhood with a father who was a country pastor. In fact, she was very critical of his cavalier approach to poetry writing. As a poet, he could be found writing extemporaneous poetry on blackboards at gatherings remarking that he was too insecure to be away from people. He invited students to share their interpretations of his poems with him. Abbe enjoyed recording his own readings of his poetry on CDs.

Francisco X. Alarcón "L.A. Prayer" (Feb. 21, 1954, Wilmington, CA –) A third-generation Californian whose family founded the Los Angeles County town of Wilmington, Alarcón moved to Guadalajara, Mexico, when he was six and started writing poetry when he was thirteen. "I wanted to transcribe the songs my grandmother used to sing. Sometimes I would forget the lines so I would make up those lines," Alacrón explains. He returned to California when he was eighteen to attend university.

Maya Angelou "Harlem Hopscotch" (b. Marguerite Ann Johnson, April 4, 1928, St. Louis, MO –) At fourteen, Angelou dropped out of school to become San Francisco's first African-American female cable car conductor. She later finished high school, giving birth to her son, Guy, a few weeks after graduation. She was given the name Maya Angelou after her debut performance as a dancer in the Purple Onion cabaret. Dr. Angelou is a celebrated poet, memoirist, novelist, educator, dramatist, producer, actress, historian, filmmaker, and civil rights activist.

Amina Baraka "The Last Word" (b. Sylvia Vanderpool, March 6, 1936, New York City – 2011) Baraka changed her name first to Sylvia Robinson and then to Amina Baraka when she married Amiri Baraka in 1967. She made her recording debut while a fourteen-year-old student at Washington Irving High School. Some claim that Baraka is the sole individual responsible for the birth of rap music.

Amiri Baraka "Wise I" (b. Everett LeRoi Jones, October 7, 1934, Newark, NJ –) Baraka graduated two years ahead of his high school class and has written essays, poems, drama, music history and criticism. Baraka was associated with the "Beat Generation" in the East Village in New York City. He is a revolutionary political activist who has recited poetry and lectured on cultural and political issues extensively in the US, the Caribbean, Africa, and Europe.

Wendell Berry "Enemies," "My Great-Grandfather's Slaves" and "Anglo-Saxon Protestant Heterosexual Men" (August 5, 1934, Port Royal, Henry County, KY –) As a young man, Berry spent time in California, New York, and Europe before returning home to Kentucky to write and to farm. Berry's message is consistent - humans must learn to live in harmony with the natural rhythms of the earth or perish. Berry told an interviewer that he cherishes his friends who were not literary or intellectual at all, who were nevertheless intelligent, mentally alive and alert, full of wonderful stories, and whose company and conversation have been indispensable to him.

Diane Burns "Sure You Can Ask Me a Personal Question" (1956, Lawrence, KS – 2006) Burns was born to a Chemehuevi father and an Anishinabe mother. In third grade she won the first-place prize for her poem, 'A Pencil Can Travel.' Burns spent her senior year of high school at the American Indian Art Institute in Santa Fe, NM, and then received a scholarship from Barnard College; her goal was to become a lawyer. Eventually, Burns gave poetry readings at the Nuyorican Poets Café in the East Village in NYC for many years.

Wanda Coleman "the ISM" (b. Wanda Evans, Nov. 13, 1946, Los Angeles, CA –) Coleman grew up in the Watts area of Los Angeles loving books. She began writing poetry as a child of five, and published her first poems in a local newspaper at age thirteen. However, Coleman never enjoyed the public schools she attended, and considered them "dehumanizing." Married and the mother of two children by age twenty, she worked many different kinds of jobs. While working days, at night and on weekends she developed her craft by attending various writing workshops in the Los Angeles area.

Billy Collins "Man in Space" (b. William James Collins, New York City, March 22, 1941 –) Billy Collins is an only child. His Canadian mother was raised on a farm; she often recited verses and cultivated in her young son the love of words, both written and spoken. His father had an active sense of humor and love of practical jokes and one-line zingers. Collins attended private schools in New York and eventually studied for his advanced degrees at California state universities. Collins served as the US Poet Laureate for two terms from 2001-2003.

Philip Dacey "The Handicapped" (May 9, 1939, St. Louis, MO –) Dacey was educated by Incarnate Word nuns and Jesuit priests for sixteen years. He served in the Peace Corps in Nigeria from 1963-1965 and taught at Miles College, Birmingham, Alabama after returning in 1966. Dacey has moved from Minnesota where he raised three children, taught at the university, and wrote poetry for many years, to the Upper West Side of Manhattan.

Enid Dame "Riding the D-Train" (b. Enid Jacobs, June 28, 1943, Beaver Falls, PA – 2003) Dame wrote poetry all of her life as a way to understand and connect with the world. She and her poet husband, Donald Lev, published a poetry magazine, "Home Planet News" for over twenty years. Dame was a Lilith scholar and her poems explored themes of urban life, Jewish history and identity, women's issues and political activism.

Toi Derricotte "St. Peter Claver" (April 12, 1941, Hamtramck, MI –) Derricotte's mother was a Louisiana Creole and her father was from Kentucky. At around ten or eleven years old, she began a secret journal. At fifteen, Derricotte showed her poetry to a cousin who told her that her poems were morbid. Derricotte felt that her Catholic upbringing was steeped in images of death and punishment. Her poetry explores deeply personal issues including gender oppression and familial strife within the black community.

Chitra Banerjee Divakaruni "Indian Movie, New Jersey" (July 29, 1956, Calcutta, India –) Divakaruni was born and lived in India until 1976, at which point she left Calcutta and came to the US. One of her earliest memories is that of her grandfather telling her stories from the ancient Indian scriptures, the *Ramayana* and the *Mahabharata*. She noticed that the main relationships the women had were with men; they never had women friends. This greatly influenced Divakaruni's writing, which focuses on women's relationships. To earn money for her education, she held many odd jobs, including babysitting and washing instruments in a science lab.

Paul Laurence Dunbar "Sympathy" (June 27, 1872, Dayton, OH – 1906) Dunbar was a turn-of-the-century literary star known for his novels, short stories, essays, and poetry. Recognized as the first African American man of letters, Dunbar was the son of ex-slaves and was raised by his widowed mother. He wrote his first poem at age six and gave his first public recital at age nine. The only black student in his class, he became Class President and Class Poet. With racial prejudice precluding him from literary positions, Dunbar worked as an elevator operator which allowed him time to write.

Ray Durem "Award" (b. Ramón Durem, 1915, Seattle, WA – 1963) At the age of fourteen Durem ran away from home to join the Navy and later became a member of the International Brigades during the Civil War in Spain. He eventually enrolled in university and joined the Communist party. During the 1940s he discovered an African American identity. Durem moved his family to Guadalajara, Mexico in order to escape government harassment. He began writing under the name of "Ray Durem" and his poetry caught the attention of Langston Hughes.

Jimmie Durham "Columbus Day" (1940, Washington, AK –) A sculptor and poet of Wolf Clan Cherokee descent, Durham was born into a family of carvers and political activists. He studied at L'École des Beaux-Arts in Geneva, Switzerland until being drawn back to the US through his involvement with the American Indian movement. Before achieving his international reputation as an artist, Durham was the director of the International Indian Treaty Council, which campaigned and negotiated for land rights. Durham lives in Rome and Berlin.

Deborah Garrison "Please Fire Me" (b. Deborah Gotleib, February 12, 1965, Ann Arbor, MI –) Garrison's father died when she was fourteen, and she and her two sisters were raised by their mother. Garrison majored in creative writing and has an advanced degree in literature. Most of her poems were written when Garrison was living in the East Village in New York City and climbing the editorial career ladder.

Gogisgi "Look Back" (b. Carroll Arnett, November 9, 1927, Oklahoma City, OK – 1997) Gogisgi was born of Cherokee-French ancestry. He served in the U.S. Marine Corps and was former Deer Clan Chief of the Overhill Band of the Cherokee Nation. Gogisgi means "Smoke" in Cherokee. A poet and professor, Gogisgi is remembered especially for his generosity to younger poets.

Guillermo Gómez-Peña "Mexico Is Sinking" (1955, Mexico City, Mexico –) Gómez-Peña was raised in Mexico City and came to the US at the age of twenty-three. His work, which includes performance art, video, audio, installations, poetry, journalism, and cultural theory, explores cross-cultural issues, immigration, the politics of language, "extreme culture" and new technologies in the era of globalization. He is a MacArthur fellow. He mixes English and Spanish, fact and fiction, social reality and pop culture, Chicano humor and activist politics. When Gómez-Peña married Emily Hicks, the groom stood in Mexico and the bride in California as they recited their vows.

Joy Harjo "Perhaps the World Ends Here" (b. Joy Foster, May 9, 1951, Tulsa, OK –) Between her mother and father, Harjo can claim Creek and Cherokee Indian, African American, Irish, and French Canadian heritage. Harjo is an enrolled member of the Muskogee Tribe. She began writing poetry when the national Indian political climate demanded singers and speakers, and was taken by the intensity and beauty possible in the craft. She took up the saxophone because she wanted to learn how to sing and play in a band that would combine the poetry with music. Harjo plays alto saxophone in a band called Poetic Justice.

Lee Herrick "jap" (December, 1970, Daejeon, South Korea –) Herrick was adopted by a Caucasian family at ten months and is the brother of an adopted older sister. He was raised in San Francisco's East Bay Area and now teaches writing and poetry at a local college. Herrick has traveled throughout El Salvador, Honduras, Guatemala, Mexico, Belize, Peru, Bolivia, Cambodia, Thailand, South Korea, China, Vietnam, and Laos. Adoption is a strong current running through his poetry. As a parent, Herrick has adopted a daughter at ten months of age from China.

Garrett Hongo "The Legend" (May 30, 1951, Volcano, Hawai'i –) Hongo is a Yonsei, a fourth generation Japanese American. He moved to California with his family when he was six years old. Hongo attended a racially mixed high school in a working-class Los Angeles neighborhood, where he was exposed to the urban street life and cultural alienation that color his work. Hongo's poetry also addresses the trials of immigrants, including the forced internment of Japanese Americans during World War II, as well as the anti-Japanese sentiment they suffer today.

Langston Hughes "Misery" (February 1, 1902, Joplin, MO – 1967) Hughes's parents divorced when he was a small child, and his father moved to Mexico. He was raised by his grandmother until he was thirteen. Hughes then moved to Lincoln, Illinois, to live with his mother and her husband, before the family eventually settled in Cleveland, Ohio. Hughes began writing poetry in the eighth grade in Lincoln, and was selected as Class Poet. He wrote novels, short stories and plays, as well as poetry, and is also known for his engagement with the world of jazz.

Phyllis Koestenbaum "Admission of Failure" (1930, Brooklyn, NY –) Koestenbaum shared with an interviewer that she did a lot of reading from a very early age. She was very silent about all the things that really mattered to her. Even in the poem it's difficult for her to express the self—although some of the poems are indeed very confessional. Her difficulty with self-expression leads her to work in forms like prose poems. She is working on a sequence of Mistranslations, poems veritably her own, since, except for a minor knowledge of French, she does not read or speak the languages of the original texts. Koestenbaum studies and writes prose poems and has been a poetry teacher for many years in California.

Abraham Lincoln "First Inaugural Address" (February 12, 1809, Sinking Spring Farm, Hardin County, Kentucky – 1865) Lincoln was raised in the Baptist church which opposed alcohol, dancing, and slavery. When he was born, his father, Thomas Lincoln, was one of the richest men in the county. Within a few years, he lost all his land in court cases. Lincoln's mother died when he was nine years old. He eventually had a stepmother with whom he became very close. Lincoln had one year of formal elementary schooling; beyond that he was self-taught and an avid reader. He did not like the hard labor of frontier life though he was tall and strong and was known to wrestle competitively with his friends. As a young man, Lincoln left home and worked in New Salem, IL, taking goods to New Orleans, LA. The story goes that after witnessing slavery firsthand in New Orleans, Lincoln walked back home.

Edwin Markham "Outwitted" and "The Greater Thing" (b. Charles Edwin Anson Markham, April 23, 1852, Oregon City, OR – 1940) Markham was the youngest of six children. His parents were divorced shortly after his birth and he saw almost nothing of his father. In 1856, Markham moved with his mother and sister to a ranch in Lagoon Valley, northeast of San Francisco. By the age of twelve, he was doing hard labor on the family farm. Markham's mother vehemently opposed his interest in literature, but he attended college nonetheless and managed to earn enough money through teaching to continue his studies.

Ellyn Maybe "Picasso" (July 10 –) Maybe self-identifies as a poet, muse, and enigma. Maybe reported in a self-interview that when she was a little girl she wrote stories. Being of low self-esteem, Maybe felt that it was too much fun so she stopped until she moved to New York City when she was twenty and the poems just arrived. She hasn't stopped writing poetry since. Maybe went to film school in Prague for two years on a Benjamin A. Gilman Scholarship from the US Department of Education. Ellyn Maybe, as the story goes, got her moniker from the sign-up sheets at open mics. Always unsure, she'd sign up as Ellyn with a "(maybe)" added to indicate that she might not read when the time came. She liked how the 'y' in Ellyn matched with the 'y' in 'maybe'. The name stuck and Maybe became a premier performance poet. The Los Angeles-based Ellyn Maybe Band was formed in 2010 after the release of the critically acclaimed album, Rodeo for the Sheepish (Hen House Studios).

Peter Meinke "A Poem to My Son Peter" (1932, Flatbush, NY –) Meinke was born in Brooklyn and moved to New Jersey where he attended high school. He wrote that one "perverse choice" he made early on was that he wanted to write poetry, "Even to myself, a young kid in Brooklyn, it seemed weird: I didn't know anyone who read it, or even liked it, but I'd spend countless night hours carried away by Louis Untermeyer's anthologies." Meinke wrote in his graduation yearbook "Wants to be: Writer; Probably will be: Censored." Meinke is a literature scholar and professor; he writes short stories and poetry.

Alice Mishkin "Other People's Lives" (1911, New York – ?) A psychologist at two New York City nursing homes compiled an oral history in the form of poetry written by the residents including Alice Mishkin who was in her eighties at the time. *Many Things to Tell You: Natural Poetry by People Living in Nursing Homes: Collection and Comment* intersperses the psychologist's comments on nursing homes and aging. Mishkin felt that older people want to talk about how they have found meaning in life through the process of coping with events in their lives.

Pat Mora "Bilingual Christmas" and "La Migra" (January 19, 1942, El Paso, TX –) Mora was raised in a bilingual family where books were an important part of her life. Family, Mexican American culture, and the desert are all important themes in Mora's writing. Mora wrote that her ideas come from the desert where she grew up — "the open spaces, wide sky, all that sun and all those animals that scurry across the hot sand or fly high over the mountains."

Ilze Mueller "Invisibility Poem: Lesbian" (b. Ilze Klavina Müller, 1951, Germany –) Mueller's family emigrated from Latvia during World War II. Pushed to learn additional languages by her father, who was never sure where they'd be moving next, she learned numerous languages even before she had completed high school. She writes about gardening, eating, and treasuring food — which was scarce during her childhood. Mueller splits her writing between translation and poetry.

Dwight Okita "In Response to Executive Order 9066" (b. Dwight Holden Okita, 1958, Chicago, IL –) Okita is Japanese American, gay, and Buddhist. His first publication came in first grade in the *Luella Log*. Okita's father was a schoolteacher and armchair philosopher and his mother was interned in a relocation camp for Japanese Americans for four years when she was a teenager. Okita lives in Chicago where he writes poetry, scripts, and fiction.

Mary Oliver "Sunrise" (September 10, 1935, Maple Heights, OH –) Oliver began writing poetry at the age of fourteen, and at seventeen visited the home of the late Pulitzer Prize winning poet Edna St. Vincent Millay, in Austerlitz, upper New York state. Oliver and Norma, the poet's sister, became friends. Oliver once told an interviewer her secret to success which was that she was very careful never to take an interesting job. For Oliver, the only worthy interest was writing. She says that she once found walking herself in the woods with no pen and went later to hide pencils in the trees so she would never be caught in that position again.

Alicia Ostriker "Windshield" (b. Alicia Suskin, November 11, 1937, Brooklyn, NY –) Ostriker grew up in a housing project in New York City where her mother read Shakespeare and Browning, among others, which inspired a love of literature in her and prompted her to write her own Jewish feminist poetry. Ostriker is a literature scholar and professor whose poetry is widely translated.

Dorothy Parker "Poem in the American Manner" (b. Dorothy Rothschild, August 22, 1893, West End, NJ – 1967) Parker was the youngest of four children. The family was rich, Jewish, and related to the Rothschild Banking clan. Parker was educated at a Catholic school. She moved to New York City, where she wrote during the day and earned money at night playing the piano in a dancing school. When Parker died in 1967, she left her estate to civil rights leader Martin Luther King, Jr.

Ishmael Reed "Points of View" (b. Ishmael Scott Reed, February 22, 1938, Chattanooga, TN –) Reed grew up in working class neighborhoods in Buffalo, New York. He attended public schools and the local university. Reed moved to New York City, where he co-founded the *East Village Other*, an underground newspaper that achieved a national reputation. In 1967, Reed's first novel was published and he moved to Berkeley, California, later relocating to Oakland, where he currently resides. Reed is a novelist, poet, playwright, essayist, publisher, editor, television producer, radio and television commentator, teacher and lecturer.

Kenneth Rexroth "Discrimination" (b. Kenneth Charles Marion Rexroth, December 22, 1905, South Bend, IN – 1982) Orphaned at fourteen, Rexroth moved in with his aunt in Chicago, where he was expelled from high school. He began publishing in magazines at the age of fifteen. He educated himself in literary salons, nightclubs, lecture halls, and hobo camps. In 1923 he served a prison term for partial ownership of a brothel. Rexroth organized and emceed the legendary Six Gallery reading on October 7, 1955, at which Allen Ginsberg introduced the world to the epic poem "Howl." While Rexroth's work was composed with attention to musical traditions, and he performed his poems with jazz musicians, he was distinctly displeased when he became known as the father of the Beats.

Luis J. Rodriguez "The News You Don't Get at Home" and "Piece by Piece" (July 4, 1954, El Paso, TX –) Rodriguez was born on the US/Mexico border and is of Mexika/Raramuri indigenous descent. At the age of two, his family migrated from Chihuahua to South Central Los Angeles. He was an active street gang member in the East LA area having joined a gang at age eleven. He began using drugs at age twelve. Rodriguez dropped out of high school and was also kicked out of his home. From ages thirteen to eighteen, he was arrested for numerous crimes, including stealing, fighting, rioting, attempted murder, and assaulting police officers. He emerged as one of the leading Chicano writers in the country with memoirs, fiction, nonfiction, children's literature, and poetry.

Assotto Saint "The Geography of Poetry" (b. Yves F. Lubin, October 2, 1957, Haiti – 1994) Saint was raised by his mother and did not meet his father until he was an adult. While visiting his mother in the US, he decided to relocate to New York. He studied pre-med in college but soon left to pursue his interests in dance and theater. It was at this time that Lubin changed his name. The decision to adopt the name of Assotto Saint was an affirmation of the writer's Haitian roots. The word "assotto" identifies a drum used in voodoo rituals, while "Saint" is a reference to Toussaint L'Ouverture, the former slave who led the revolt against French colonial rule in Haiti. Saint was the lead singer in a techno pop duo band, Xotika. Their dance song, "Forever Gay" was released in Feeding the Flame by Flying Fish Records. Saint died of AIDS-related complications.

Tupac Shakur "Liberty Needs Glasses" (b. Lesane Parish Crooks, 1971, Harlem, NY – 1996) Shakur's mother was a member of the Black Panther Party. She renamed him Tupac Amaru Shakur in 1972 after Tupac Amaru, an Inca who was sentenced to death by the Spaniards. Tupac Amaru, in the Inca language, means "shining serpent". Shakur studied dance including ballet. When he was twelve years old, his mother enrolled him in Harlem's 127th St Ensemble. He played Travis in "A Raisin in The Sun" in his first acting role. He was offered a record contract at the age of thirteen. However, his mother refused to let him sign anything at such a young age. Along with friends, he founded the "Junior Black Panthers." By the time he was twenty, Shakur had been arrested eight times, even serving eight months in prison after being convicted of sexual abuse. Shakur recorded close to 150 songs during the final year of his life, and often completed three songs per day. More of his music has been released since his death than while he was alive.

Gary Soto "Failing in the Presence of Ants" (April 12, 1952, Fresno, CA –) Soto grew up in the barrio and has borrowed from that community to create an astonishing number of works. After Soto's father's death, the family moved to a rough neighborhood in an industrial area. As Soto and his siblings grew older, they worked in the fields and factories. Education was not part of their culture—the culture of poverty. Although Soto was not encouraged to read at home, he was exploring the world of books on his own at the school library. Soto stumbled upon the works of Chilean poet Pablo Neruda. He commented in an interview that he wanted to do this thing called writing poetry.

William Stafford "A Ritual to Read to Each Other", "Freedom of Expression" and "Being a Person" (January 17, 1914, Hutchison, KS – 1993) Stafford was the oldest of three children in a highly literate family. During the Depression, his family moved around in any effort to find work for his father. Stafford contributed to family income by working in the sugar beet fields and working as an electrician's mate. Stafford was a conscientious objector in World War II. One of the most unusual aspects of his career is that he began publishing his poetry later in life. His first collection of poetry was published when he was forty-eight years old.

Carmen Tafolla "Marked" (1951, San Antonio, TX –) Tafolla was told by her junior high school principal that she had potential to make it all the way to high school. She did, and followed it with a B.A., an M.A., and a Ph.D. Tafolla has remarked that her elementary school did not have a library and her public library was two miles from her home. An internationally acclaimed Chicana writer and educational consultant, Tafolla is the author of nonfiction, screenplays, poetry, and numerous short stories, academic articles, and children's books.

Natasha Trethewey "White Lies" (April 26, 1966, Gulfport, MS –) Before she started grade school, Trethewey's parents divorced and she moved to Decatur, Georgia, with her mother. As a youth, Trethewey spent her summers with her grandmother in Mississippi and in New Orleans with her father who is a poet. She has always loved words and even at a young age spent much of her time in a library reading as many books as possible. When Trethewey was nineteen, her mother passed away. Trethewey is a literature scholar and professor of creative writing. Trethewey was named Poet Laureate by the Library of Congress in 2012.

Fawaz Turki "Being a Good *Americani*" (1941, Haifa, Palestine –) Turki is a Palestinian American poet, essayist, author and commentator. He grew up as a refugee in Beirut after his family fled Palestine during the Arab-Israeli War of 1948. His childhood was spent in a refugee camp and on the streets of Beirut, followed by years spent in Australia, France, and the US in search of his identity, both personal and national. In describing this journey, Turki also relates the stories of family, friends, and comrades, those who fought the battles and those who walked away from them.

Nancy Byrd Turner "Immigrants" (July 29, 1880, Boydton, Mecklenburg County, VA – 1971)
Turner was a descendent of both Thomas Jefferson and Pocohantas. Through her father's family
she was related to Jefferson, and through her mother's side her ancestry was traced to Pocohantas.
Turner had begun writing poetry at an early age; by age twenty-two, her poems were being
published regularly in national magazines. Turner was a poet, novelist, editor, lyricist for children's
songs, and lecturer.

Louis Untermeyer "Prayer" (October 1, 1885, New York City, NY – 1977) After a brief formal
education, Untermeyer left high school without graduating and found work in his father's jewelry
manufacturing company. Untermeyer was very interested in literature and in 1911 he published
his first book of poetry. He also held left-wing political views and was the literary editor of the
Marxist journal, *The Masses.* By 1923 Untermeyer was vice-president in his father's company
but he decided to resign and concentrate on writing. Over the next fifty years he wrote, edited or
translated over one hundred books.

Walt Whitman "Leaves of Grass" (May 31, 1819, Huntington, Long Island, NY – 1892) Walter
was called Walt to distinguish him from his father, Walter Whitman Sr. Walt was the second
of nine children who moved frequently in their youth due to bad investments. Whitman left
school at eleven and started working for printers to add income for his family. He wrote, taught,
and eventually founded his own newspaper, as he was keenly interested in politics. While
biographers often debate Whitman's sexuality, everyone agrees that *Leaves of Grass* is a significant
contribution to American literature. Whitman wanted to write an epic poem for the everyman.
First published in 1855, Whitman continued to tinker with it until his death in 1892.

Mitsuye Yamada "Warning," (b. Mitsuye Yasutake, July 5, 1923, Fukuoka, Japan –) Yamada was
raised in Seattle, Washington (her parents were visiting Japan when she was born) until 1942
when she and her family were interned in Minidoka, Idaho, a US internment camp for Japanese
American citizens and resident aliens. Yamada and her brother were allowed to leave the camp to
attend college where she studied literature. Yamada became a naturalized US citizen in 1955. She
considers herself Nisei (second-generation Japanese American). Yamada is a Japanese American
activist, feminist, essayist, poet, author, editor, and literature professor.

Credits

George Abbe, "Possessor's Pity" Reprinted courtesy of Branden Books, Boston.

Francisco X. Alarcón, "L.A. Prayer" from *From the Other Side of Night/Del otro lado de la noche: New and Selected Poems,* by Francisco X. Alarcón, copyright © 2002 Francisco X. Alarcón. Reprinted by permission of the University of Arizona Press.

Maya Angelou, "Harlem Hopscotch", from JUST GIVE ME A COOL DRINK OF WATER 'FORE I DIE by Maya Angelou, copyright © 1971 by Maya Angelou. Used by permission of Random House, Inc.

Amina Baraka, "The Last Word" by Amina Baraka, copyright © 1994 by Amina Baraka, from UNSETTLING AMERICA by Maria Mazziotti Gillan and Jennifer Gillan. Used by permission of Viking Penguin, a division of Penguin Group (USA) Inc.

Amiri Baraka, "Wise I" from *Transbluesency: The selected poems of Amiri Baraka/LeRoi Jones.* Reprinted by permission of SLL/Sterling Lord Literistic, Inc. Copyright by Amiri Baraka.

Wendell Berry, "Enemies" and "Anglo-Saxon Protestant Heterosexual Men" from ENTRIES: POEMS by Wendell Berry, copyright © 1994 by Wendell Berry. Used by permission of Pantheon Books, a division of Random House, Inc.

Wendell Berry, "My Great Grandfather's Sleeves" Copyright © 1984 by Wendell Berry from *The Collected Poems of Wendell Berry,* 1957-1982. Reprinted by permission of Counterpoint.

Wanda Coleman, "the ISM" is reprinted with permission from the author.

Billy Collins, "Man in Space" from *The Art of Drowning,* by Billy Collins, copyright © 1995. Reprinted by permission of the University of Pittsburgh Press.

Philip Dacey, "The Handicapped" by Philip Dacey is reprinted from *Night Shift at the Crucifix Factory* (University of Iowa Press, 1991) by permission of the author.

Enid Dame, "Riding the D-Train" is reprinted with permission from West End Press.

Toi Derricotte, "St. Peter Claver" from *Captivity,* by Toi Derricotte, © 1989. Reprinted by permission of the University of Pittsburgh Press.

Chitra Banerjee Divakaruni, "Indian Movie, New Jersey" Copyright © by Chitra Banerjee Divakaruni. Reprinted by permission of the author and the Sandra Dijkstra Literary Agency.

Jimmie Durham, "Columbus Day" is reprinted with permission from West End Press.

Deborah Garrison, "Please Fire Me", copyright © 1998 by Deborah Garrison, from A WORKING GIRL CAN'T WIN AND OTHER POEMS by Deborah Garrison. Used by permission of Random House, Inc.

Guillermo Gómez-Peña, "Mexico is Sinking", Copyright © 1994 by Guillermo Gómez-Peña. First published in *High Performance,* no. 35, 1986. Reprinted by permission of *High Performance.*

Joy Harjo, "Perhaps the World Ends Here", from THE WOMAN WHO FELL FROM THE SKY by Joy Harjo. Copyright © 1994 by Joy Harjo. Used by permission of W.W. Norton & Company, Inc.

Index

About Our Contributors

COMMON, born Lonnie Rashid Lynn Jr., is the son of Dr. Mahalia Ann Hines, noted Chicago educator, and Lonnie Lynn, a former professional basketball player. He writes, "my truth is this: I inherited love and trouble, joy and fear. I experienced all of these things before I could even put them into words." COMMON is a hip hop artist and MC, poet, actor, producer, designer, author, and social activist. But most importantly to COMMON, he is the proud father of his daughter, Omoye.

Gail Bush is a graduate of the Chicago Public Schools. Her academic background includes anthropology, library science, and educational psychology. Bush is a professor of education and lives with her family in Evanston, Illinois.

Randy Meyer grew up in Anaheim, California. He has been an editor and writer in the library and educational journal and book publishing fields in New York and Chicago. Meyer is a middle school librarian and lives with his family in Somerville, Massachusetts.